CW00358202

KINGDOM OF TRUTH

This work was first published in Great Britain by white Flag in 2011.

The right of Abigrael Halo-Hymn to be identified as the Author of the Work has been asserted by white Flag limited in accordance with the Copyright, Designs and Patents Act 1988.

50   49   48   47   46   45   44   43   42   41

ISBN 978-0-9553598-3-5

Cover design by: white Flag limited
Printed by: CPI Group (UK) Ltd., Croydon, CR0 4YY
Typesetting by: white Flag limited

Readability Statistics

Counts

Words	14347
Characters	92565
Paragraphs	437
Sentences	550

Averages

Sentences per Paragraph	1.9
Words per Sentence	24.8
Characters per Word	4.3

Readability

Passive Sentences	20%
Flesch Reading Ease	64
Flesch-Kincard Grad Level	10

KINGDOM OF TRUTH

BY
ABIGRAEL HALO-HYMN

THE KINGDOM

CONTENTS

PART ONE – INTRODUCING KNOWLEDGE

PART TWO: ESTABLISHING TRUST

PART THREE: INAUGURATING 'THE' KINGDOM

PART FOUR: ETERNALIZING 'THE' LAW

PART ONE
INTRODUCING KNOWLEDGE

THE COMMON DEMON-HATER

The history of mankind has one single attribute that has repeated itself relentlessly. Every nation, country, creed, tribe and civilisation has had power structures where there are ruling elite and the few control the many.

However, there was one nation that, for some several hundred years, did not have a power structure; and if it was not for this nation we would not have had the opportunity to observe an alternative way of living. This nation is still with us today and, though they have adopted a power structure against the wishes of their patron, we owe them an immense sense of gratitude because they allow us to see the realistic possibility of having a utopian society.

The nation to which I am referring to is Israel and the patron of this nation is the creator of the universe. This is not to say that Israel is a utopian island amid the sea of troubled nations – for they now have a power structure and a government which elects one man to rule over other men; just like all the other nations. However, there was a time they had the perfect way of life which was with us from the moment they received the law until they elected a king; and this was done against the wishes of their patron - God.

Fortunately for them, God did not forsake them for doing this, and he told them he will spare them for his own names sake. He used this terminology because he plans to establish his own kingdom and this booklet will outline the exact nature of the coming Kingdom Of Yahweh.

NOTES

THE (NOT SO) NEW WORLD ORDER

Any nation (government) would argue they have the correct blue-print for a sophisticated civilisation; and with their belief, they would insist their setup would bring about utopia if every nation / country would copy their ideals. Indeed, we need only look to the modern era of globalisation to see how there is a consensus of men (the ruling elite of today) who are attempting to bring these nations / countries to emulate the same principles by which they want us to live by.

The world is rapidly becoming ordered in what they call the new way of living. However, the truth is: this new world order is exactly the same as every nation / civilisation that is, or has ever been, on the face of the Earth.

The only difference is: the people who are in control are different – even if they claim do to have divine birth right to rule the world – as they have done throughout history. The Old World Order was Pax Romana - during the time Rome had peace in their province - and it is their hope to re-establish this system of government.

There is no doubt, there are many people around the world who have been made aware of the growing reality that the world is quickly moving toward a one world government where people will be treated like cattle, but there is a lack of wisdom for this knowledge; and they are in real danger of falling victim to the next whim or fad that comes along to distract their minds.

While it may appear to be a noble pursuit to have a system where we have one government with one language and one religion that uses one system of legal tender there are serious flaws to the system that this booklet will address.

NOTES

_____
_____
_____
_____
_____
_____
_____
_____
_____
_____
_____
_____

GROWING TENSION

The world is increasingly growing in opposition against the nation of Israel because the media is constantly bombarding us with images of conflict (and propaganda) that are placing the nation at the centre of all the issues in the world.

As the ruling elite begin to reveal their true intentions, the nation of Israel will become increasingly important to what happens in the world; because every person on this planet will be affected by what will transpire. Given the fact Israel is the only nation that has ever had a true utopian way of life – they have something to teach us.

The question is: what?

Whatever your sentiments regarding Israel, it is important to keep an open mind to understand exactly why the nation exists and what it means for you. You may be pleasantly surprised and filled with a bewildering sense of hope and joy after you have read what is in store for mankind. At this point I'd like to make it clear, I am not: a prophet, or messenger or an apostle; nor have I been assigned any task appointed by a deity here, as these titles would violate my own conscience. I do, however, consider myself a true and loyal friend of the creator of the universe whose name is known by the nation of Israel as: Hashem; Elohim or Yahweh.

In the Kingdom of God, there will be no flags that distinguish one nation from another for the whole world will belong to the creator and every person will live in eternal joy – like the angels in heaven – without temptation, illness or death.

NOTES

OF GREATNESS AND FAITH

The first thing we need to do here – is establish the origin of Israel.

Some several thousand years ago there was a man named Abram who was asked by his father to tend his shop, of idols, while he ran some errands. Upon his return, he found all, save the largest, of the idols smashed and when his father inquired as to what happened Abram told him the largest idol smashed all the small ones.

Naturally his father was angered and he said: this was absurd because the idols were lifeless. Abram replied: it was absurd to worship something that was lifeless.

The point here is: Abram was willing to stand up for an unpopular truth in a society that believed there were many gods which could be characterized as idols made by the hands of men. I try to imagine the pressure he must have felt to capitulate with the cultural belief of many gods; and it seems obvious he was an enlightened man with a malleable attitude that caught the attention of the great creator at this moment.

So God (who is the almighty creator of the universe), approached Abram and started a friendship with him by making several promises which have been honoured.

One such promise included: *I will curse all those who curse your descendants and bless all those who bless your descendants.*

This is the reason why your sentiments toward Abram's descendants are important. If you curse the nation of Israel and you will be cursed – if you bless them and you will be blessed. I don't know about you, but I know plenty of people who have experienced these vicissitudes – both for the better and for the worse and their sentiments on Abram's descendants were prevalent each time.

If you think these words sound like vows from a wedding: you'd be right on the money – so you should be wondering about your invitation because the coming kingdom is described as a wedding where everyone is invited.

Yes, that means you and everyone you love including those you have a grievance with are invited – and this booklet will reveal the path that will lead to the gate by which you enter. It's up to you if you want to make your way to the gate because walking the path requires a friendship with the creator which you will know is real when life appears to be filled with wonder – even when things go wrong.

FATHER OF NATIONS

A good point to make here is the fact Abram was the father of two sons that both became great nations – and God told Abram to name his sons accordingly. Ishmael (*which means God listens*) and Isaac (*which means laughter*).

After Ishmael was born God changed Abram's (*great one*) name to Abraham (*father of nations*) and Sarai's (*princess*) name to Sarah (*queen*). Ishmael is the Arab (Muslim) people and Isaac is the Israeli (Jewish) people.

Isaac (the second born of Abraham but first born of Sarah) gave birth to a son named Jacob and it is here the account of Israel begins when God makes a covenant with him and instructs him to change his name to Israel. God named him Israel because he had prevailed after striving with God and men.

Between (the days of) Abram and Israel there are many interesting facets of friendship shared between God and Abraham that tell us so much about God and his nature. For example: God asked Abraham 'Do you believe?' when he told him, at the age of ninety-nine, his descendents would number more than the stars. Abraham was counted righteous because he believed. So the idea of living-by-faith was also born at this moment in time.

Don't get me wrong – this would have been a universal truth from the very beginning. The point I'm making here is: this is when scripture first mentions we live by faith – and the importance of (appropriate) sacrifice was fully established. I use the word appropriate because sacrifice has a specific purpose that has become more personal through the ages.

NOTES

NOTES

PART TWO
ESTABLISHING TRUST

SACRIFICE OF (THE) SELF

Before God established a covenant with Abraham – God expected sacrifice (as we saw with Cain and Abel) but He never gave much explanation as to what sacrifice was all about. During the formative years of mankind's existence the general idea behind sacrifice was the offer of sacrifice (the blood of innocence usually) to please the gods in the hope they would favour the person (people) making the sacrifice.

Although God asked Abraham to sacrifice his own son – it was never his intention to actually let him do this – so when God tells his prophets (later) the idea of sacrificing children never crossed his mind He meant the sacrifice of children never entered His mind as a means to prove faithfulness or cleansing of sin.

When God said to Adam: '*Your son will save mankind.*' He was not saying the sacrifice of a son was what He wanted people to make for He knew a man would offer himself as the ultimate sacrifice to prove that self-sacrifice is rewarded by God in abundance. I'm not saying: we should endeavour to live a suicidal way of life. The scripture is clear enough about this issue. It tells us we should treat others as we would wish to be treated and use the wisdom God gives us to ensure our own survival is not compromised.

The purpose of sacrifice is to show faith by destroying something of value; and this requirement has remained with us right up to this day. However, the means and method of sacrifice have been refined.

To make sure the necessity of sacrifice is fully appreciated – I will explain why it is required of us.

The story of God is thwarted with unfathomable sadness – because man is so intent on living wickedly and a person can only grasp how He feels when they lose something of value. For example: If someone loses a loved one (say their child was killed in an accident) they will know how it felt for God to have lost his original creation.

This happened when the first man (and woman – who was created with the express intention of providing Adam with a helper that was equal to man) fell from grace after disobeying Him and became subject to death. This caused God deep sadness and this is why we are required to make sacrifice.

God wants us to have empathy for His loss to forges a friendship with Him.

DEATH MAY DIE

If you think ill of God for letting innocent people (children) die, you should remember he doesn't want anyone to die. If he didn't care – he wouldn't have bothered to tell us to not eat the forbidden fruit. He did say it would lead to death if we ate it and now that we have it in our midst we shouldn't blame him for it being here. Notice: I am referring to (it) as a thing. This is because death can be destroyed and God has a plan to remove it from our midst forever.

The other aspect of death is: it forces us to consider God and His words. I call this an awesome tool of judgement and it amazes me when I consider how powerful this is when you realise death is just an illusion at the end of the day.

Death (as explained in scripture) is: being without the knowledge of God.

WELCOME HOME (*Revision Of: Footprints*)

I died and found my friend God waiting for me at the end of a long beach where, I saw, there was just one track of footprints.

When I enquired of the prints, God explained they represented the path I had walked in life.

I felt abashed there was only a single track of prints and inquired if He had carry me, or if He had allowed me to wander alone, all my life.

God replied: '*You walked perfectly my son. You placed each footstep within my prints like a child – and that is why you see but one set of prints that start from your spiritual birth.*'

Author: Abigrael Halo-Hymn

NOTES

JUDGE MEANT – TO – DELIVER

Contrary to popular belief – judgement is not punishing the wicked. Judgement is: bringing someone to the knowledge of God.

The good shepherd does not use scare tactics (a dog) to round up the sheep. A good shepherd uses love (the bonding at birth technique) to lead his sheep safely. Have you ever seen a shepherd in the Middle East use a dog? This means that anyone who tries to scare you with talk of hell or the devil is not a good shepherd.

How do we obtain full knowledge of God?

Keep the Commandments and meditate on His precepts. That means reading the scriptures for yourself and pondering on their meaning. The Hebrew Bible, New Testament, Nag Hammadi and The Qur'ān will elevate your knowledge – wisdom and understanding. What's important is you study these texts for yourself and let them speak to you personally (as it were) without allowing any individual the opportunity to obscure the truth you now know that power-structure is unholy.

This is allowing the Holy Spirit to work with you to bring you to understand the scripture as God intended it to be understood – through humility.

Remember God chose Abram (who became Abraham) to speak to us and we should honour this by reading the scripture He has endeavoured to bring us.

D-EVIL – POWER-LUST

Does the devil exist? Truth here is: I don't know, and I don't care to know. I think it's more important to take responsibility for your own actions and ignore any temptations that come your way, than it is to worry about the demons that work tirelessly to destroy mankind. If you ask Yeshua (the Christ) for his assistance, he will help you fight against temptation and grow strong enough to fight it yourself.

Ignoring temptation renders the devil non-existent so you have the power to make him non-existent. Sounds too difficult to get your head around – try this: you cannot commit sin (even in a dream) when you have full knowledge of God. So I would highly recommend learning as much as you can about God and this booklet is a good starting point.

The criteria I use (or what I ask myself) when I'm reading or discussing religion or meditating on the subject is: does what I'm hearing, reading or thinking; glorify God? If it does: it is true – if it does not: it is a lie. This may sound rather simple – but don't be fooled into thinking this might be flawed in some way.

white Flag limited   21   www.white-flag.net

HELL – ETERNAL SUFFERING

Death is an illusion. The people you know who have died are asleep awaiting (in Sheol or the grave) the day of the Lord when they will be risen and given a new body to learn how to live in obedience to God being filled with unending joy – everlasting. This time (now) is given to Christ to find a sufficient number of saints that will assist him during the millennial rule to usher in the Kingdom of God.

There is a second death mentioned in scripture which is only administered to those who refuse to accept the sovereignty of God during what's referred to as the millennial rule of Christ – but they are not subject to the fires of an eternal hell. The idea here is: having suffered the sting of the first death people will be deterred from going through that (brief torment) again, and make the effort to walk the path to the Kingdom of God. The second death is final: but God wants everyone to love him eternally as he intends to (and will) love them eternally. Those who die the second time will not suffer eternally in a tormenting hell – they will leave existence and even their memory will be erased forever.

What's peculiar about this is: the die-hard power-lusting individuals will probably welcome this alternative. I'd hazard a guess Hitler is one of them – but even he will have the opportunity to realise his mistakes and learn to love God. You never know – it could happen.

One thing is for sure – it'll be an interesting time during the millennial rule, and I hope to be (there) beside Yeshua where we can work together.

NOTES

PART THREE
INAGURATING THE KINGDOM

ISRAEL – TRUE CALLING

What happened immediately after God made his covenant with Israel?

Scripture tells us He closed the womb of Rachel because (we are told) Jacob loved her so much. This would imply He was punishing Jacob for loving her faithfully because they did think He was punishing them for a time.

However, if we look closely at what transpired, we discover Jacob (Israel) had several sons from several wives before Rachel conceived him sons. This would strongly suggest that God (in his wisdom) knew Israel needed to have several genetic markers if he was to father a nation and closing the womb ensured this would happened. This also proves that God was (is) mindful of the necessity for extra genetic markers if the world was to be populated in the beginning; and it is likely He would have catered for this when Adam and Eve were cast out of the garden.

This also brings to our attention the true nature of the story of creation.

The story of creation is not about creating the world, the heavens and man etc. but the introduction of God and his laws to man. This also strengthens the idea that a person becomes a man / woman when he / she have knowledge of God and only through faith can they hope to live. So we know that the beginning was a time when God attempted to introduce his laws but they were met with lack of interest save a small number of people – i.e. Enoch, Noah, Abraham (which we can see now is the genealogical righteous seed of Adam and Eve).

Abel understood the requirements of sacrifice and though Cain killed Abel God knew it was because he wanted His favour. This meant even the wicked could find a way to righteousness – after all, he wanted His favour. So even with the worst of people (like Cain), God could see there was hope to bring all his creation to love Him as He loves them. With this, God saw He had to create a means by which everyone could come to Him through faith and learn of is personality (character) without compromising His own holiness.

I stand in awe when I observe His efforts through the ages and in modern times.

When He saw Abram defy the traditional legacy of his forefathers (and refused to worship idols) He realised He had an opportunity to deliver His message of love and hope to the world through his descendents. This is why you hear of Israel being referred to as God's witnesses. They (in many ways) prove God exists if you take the time to study their history and culture.

By now, you should be getting a real picture of the amount of work God has done to keep His creation in one piece without causing Himself unnecessary suffering. Yes – I did say 'suffering'.

If you think God has never suffered – you haven't been paying attention. When I look at history – I see my friend God taking refuge from the slime He sees everywhere. In fact, my heart sinks at the thought of how much He has endured.

Anyway, with the birth of the twelve sons (tribes) of Israel they grew in multitude and began to live prosperously in the land God had given them. And for a while they (the people) became a sanctuary for God until they began to ignore His commandments.

Note: the people are described as a sanctuary at this time. This means the reference to 'many mansions in the house of God' is referring to the multitude of attitudes that God can visit and the forging of correct attitudes is what scripture is designed to achieve. God is somewhat sensitive to our behaviour and He finds it difficult to tolerate wickedness and iniquity – as if you didn't know this already.

Imagine seeing flashes of rape scenes on daytime television and you might get an idea how difficult it is for God to deal with sin in the world. Getting drunk, or saying white lies to keep the peace, or (legal) sexual conquest, may seem harmless to you but this sort of behaviour disgusts God and sickens Him the way you might feel about child abuse.

How would you stop these images from being broadcast onto your television?

Would you turn the television off and hope they never comes back, or would you contact the broadcasters and complain of their offensive nature to ensure they are never displayed again? Wherever God has looked at the world, He has seen all kinds of iniquity and He has tried to deal with this in much the same way.

God has asked – even pleaded with – his creation (using prophets) to stop behaving wickedly and keep the commandments.

What would you do if the broadcasters ignored you and the law was unable to stop them? Would you destroy the television studio? This is exactly what God has done throughout history. When people ignore His prophets He exacts a wrathful, destructive and decisive end to their iniquity. Sodom and Gomorrah come to mind immediately but there are many others cities and whole nations where He shows us He refuses to tolerate wicked behaviour. If you think successful sexual conquest is something to be admired – be warned. The idea of sexual conquest is repulsive to God – in fact any sexual activity that does not lead to the creation of life is considered an abomination.

God does not discriminate against any particular type of sexuality because all forms of sexual immorality are a violation of the Royal Law.

Every form of violation of the Royal Law (in any guise) is rooted in one desire and that is the lust for power. Scripture tells us: the root of all evil is the love of money and the love of money is – the lust for power. The lust for power is the impetus for the creation of all evil in the world and Israel is the only means we have to identify this truth. This is the *real* reason why the world is slowly being drawn against Israel. The world is seeking to destroy this nation because if they are removed – the truth about the possibility for true utopia (where everyone is considered equal) can be erased from history forever and man will continue to have ruling elite where oppression will remain unchecked.

There's a lot riding on this – so it's important to pay close attention.

NOTES

UTOPIAN ENDURANCE

The nation of Israel had conquered many kingdoms and secured a land where they could honour God accordingly – with the help of their God.

During the early years of Israel's existence, scripture describes how the nation was required to cleanse them of sin on a yearly basis. They were to achieve this by undertaking specific sacrifices that the priests were to administer according to the rituals described by God (through the prophets). They kept these rituals religiously, for centuries, until 70 AD when the temple was destroyed. The nation moved quickly to emphasis on the scholarly way to enlightenment and cleansing because their means of administrating the sacrifices was compromised.

This is not to say sacrifice became unnecessary because God wants people to know what the loss of something valued feels like in order to establish empathy between the creator and His creation (at a profound level). This is the basis of the friendship God wants to establish with everyone, and I will be discussing this at greater length later. The most important aspect of the nation of Israel (that seems to have been overlooked) is the time they dwelled in the land without a king.

God instructed the people (each tribe) to set up their camps facing north, south, east and west with a tabernacle in the centre for the arc of the covenant where He would reside Himself. One of the tribes, Levi, were instructed not possess any land as they would administer the priestly duties of God. There is no mention of any power structure here and this is (probably) when God had the most joyful and peaceful time throughout the history of the world while the gentiles had a ruling class.

Although God exists beyond time and He can move to and fro between periods of time, He still needs to exist within a time frame when He deals with His creation.
For example: although He can tell Adam about Christ He is limited to the amount of information He can divulge about him and as such He is limited to the type of conversation He can have with him. Indeed, scripture does inform us God told Adam of a son he would have that would save all of mankind but He does not tell him anything about how and when. The reason why God was (is) limited to the amount of information He could (can), divulge was (is) because there were (are) dark principalities that are (is) working to destroy all of mankind.

When I read scripture I see a perfectly crafted message that is designed to bring everyone to the knowledge of God. Anyone who reads scripture with the attitude they know better will encounter a myriad of confusing contradictions that will (if they have a genuine heart) challenge their haughty forwardness. This is to say – if you do encounter any contradictions in scripture, you should remember it is your own perception that is flawed and not scripture. God has worked tirelessly (and flawlessly) to help His creation draw the conclusion we need Him and His love to live eternally with Him.

Would you help a rapist or a murderer change his / her ways?

God would, for He doesn't want to forsake anyone. Even after death, He wants everyone to come to the full knowledge of His ways during what's called the millennial rule of Christ (returned). Surely this proves He cares if He is willing to endure such dirty work to bring you and everyone else the means to attain eternal life. I mean – why else would He bother to do all He has done through Israel.

This time (with the nation of Israel – before they had a king) was important for God because it gave Him a place to rest while He continued to work on bringing the word (truth) to mankind. Most of his work was done through prophets but there were (are) occasions when He takes a more direct approach – as with the destruction of wicked nations for example; or meeting faithful servants who have documented His-story.

NOTES

IN THE WAKE OF A DREAM

King Nebuchadnezzar awoke one morning and remembered a vivid dream he had. He demanded his sages told him what the dream was and what it meant. Naturally, none of them could and they faced execution for their failure. Fortunately, for them, there was a servant of God in the king's services (as a chief eunuch) that heard of the request and he offered to oblige him. His name was Daniel and he explained the dream represented the stages of mankind's history.

Daniel explained the dream was a statue of a man with a head of gold, breastplate of silver, thighs of bronze, legs of iron and feet of iron and clay. A rock, not forged of hand, smashed the feet and caused the content of the whole image to blow in the wind like chaff. Daniel then explained the meaning of the dream: the gold represented his own kingdom, which would be conquered by the next super-power that used silver as weapons. This super-power would then be conquered by a kingdom that uses bronze and they in turn would be conquered by a super-power that uses iron as weapons.

The final stage (the feet of iron and clay) represented a time when a super-power would be fragmented and unable to find accord (such as we see with the European Union now). The stone was used by God to destroy the rule of man and set up the Kingdom of God. The important thing here is to understand the symbolism behind the image and who the conquering powers are.

The stages are the following:

1) Gold – Babylon (soft component).
2) Silver – Persia (medium component).
3) Bronze – Greece (tough component).
4) Iron – Rome (hard component).
5) Clay & Iron – Europe (malleable and hard components).
6) Giant Rock – Return of Christ and His Saints.

The point here is to note how the different components get harder each time as the conquering super-powers advance on the next.

Now I realise this may seem rather obvious but what isn't so obvious is the mention of clay – because there are other elements that will not mix with iron that could have been used to explain the same thing. The mention of clay has a greater meaning and it is important to ascertain what. If we look to the word clay in scripture we can see it is used to describe how God created Adam. I do not know if Adam was literally made of clay but it does strongly suggest God works as a potter to develop individuals.

This then also explains that the dream has a deeper meaning in that it shows how man becomes ever more difficult to work with as he indoctrinates his own rules to set up and establish the power structures we see today. The point here is what does clay represents in the dream. If clay is what a potter needs to create his pots – I would say the modern day has people that are willing to find new ways of living without power-structure and this is why I believe you are reading this booklet right now. It would be wrong of me to tell you how to live your life but you should ask yourself – if my life is in the hands of God, am I clay, or am I one of the metals with different grades of malleability?

When I say 'in the hands of God' – I do not mean: listening to what a priest in a church says for they are men / women who accept the power structure that has created the church, that is recognised by secular rule, we see today. Remember: any kind of power structure is in opposition to everything God stands for. This isn't to say: the Priests in a church or the Clerics in a mosque or the Rabbi's in a synagogue are evil. They are (as far as I have observed) doing the best they can to serve God. Some may be aware that the Kingdom Of God will (does) not have a power structure and they have convinced themselves they are preparing the groundwork for the Lord's great day as they work within the power structure that has been put in place by their – trusted – predecessors.

Power structure is the opposite of the Kingdom Of God. I do not recommend approaching them to challenge them with what you have learned hear because you need to remember each individual has different levels of malleability and it is important for you to do all you can to be as clay.

A priest is in receipt of an income they will be reluctant to relinquish, so they are more likely to be one of the metals and they will use all the false knowledge (doctrine) they have (believe) to support their belief they are serving God correctly. I will talk more about this false knowledge along with the dark principalities later and give you examples of how they refuse to see the obvious. Such false knowledge (doctrine) has proven to be a powerful force in the world because it secures a basis of faith for the haughty. The idea being: if they can't understand something – it is where their faith exists. There is nothing more frustrating than trying to talk to someone who thinks that being without knowledge is (faith) a prerequisite for entry into the kingdom – they are wrong and they are, all too often, shackled by their own perfidious and froward attitude.

It is more important to remember the reason why you are reading this booklet and that is because you want to know what the Kingdom Of God will be like.

This kingdom will come when the large rock (described in the dream) destroys mans rule and Yeshua will set-up the Kingdom of God. The thing you need to know here is what happens to clay when it is put through the fire (of brimstone as described in revelation). I think we would all agree here, it sets hard and assumes a permanent shape. Permanent shape sounds physical in nature but I am talking spiritually here and this is where I start to talk about spiritual matters including the dark principalities I have mentioned several times in this booklet.

NOTES

PART FOUR
ESTABLISHING "THE" LAW

RESCUE (ME) MY RÉSUMÉ

I was intrigued by the phrase Yeshua stated: '*There will be others that will come after myself who will be greater than I.*' The world (including the spiritualists), have totally fallen into the trap of thinking he is telling them there is a power structure in heaven which has been characterized by the phrase '*There are many mansions in my house*'.

I have already explained the 'mansions' phrase is referring to attitudes, and I can confirm to you now Yeshua was telling us there will be people who will reach greater numbers of people with the technology we have available now.

Temptation – what is it? Remember: the root of all evil is the love of money and the love of money is the lust for power.

This can exist very subtly within – for example you may want to be a manager within a company without realising the responsibilities this position carries. You may like the idea of telling others what to do or ordering people around may seem perfectly normal to you. Truth is: this attitude (which the tyrants of the past have also shared) is the reason why mankind has fallen into such dark times through its history and why people are yearning for something different now.

Remember Ishmael means: 'God is listening' and God advised Abraham that every man's hand would be against him – this means whenever we see conflict and we feel dismayed by the violence we see in the world today we can be reassured God can hear us groaning and He cares.

Where does lust for power exist? Put simply: it exists in the heart.

You may enjoy playing the game of sexual conquest but this is the lust for power over another individual. You may enjoy getting drunk but this too is about seizing the power you have to remain conscious and this has provided the wicked an opportunity to be iniquitous claiming they did not know what they were doing at the time. How many times has a drinker said: 'It wasn't me?' The truth is – they knew before they started drinking what their intentions were (tendencies are).

Some alcoholics may have a genuine addiction which might have started when they wanted to escape the reality they find themselves in. I should point out here: they would not have any turmoil in their lives if they kept the commandments from the start. This doesn't mean they are bad or can't succeed – it's just going to be harder for them to live a life of sobriety when Yeshua arrives with his saints.

This is what the dark principalities are working to do. They are trying to fill you with so much nonsense and ideas about correct ways to live your life you will find it hard (like the recovering alcoholic) during the millennial rule.

If everyone kept the commandments we would all live in harmony – and there would never be a need to teach our children not to talk to strangers.

There's little point is saying: 'Why should I bother – everyone else is out to get what they can;' because Yeshua **will** return and then you will be faced with the option of dying again (for the last time) or living in the kingdom where everyone **will** keep the commandments. If you decide you want to live in the kingdom (forever) then it would be wise to go 'cold turkey' while you still have the chance in this life. Yeshua did say if we keep the commandments to the end we would not taste the sting of death.

The dark principalities are demonic in nature and they need somewhere to reside – within the mind. One way this is created (by willing participants of evil such as the creators of power structures – the illuminate and freemasons) is to cause trauma to children. When a child of about five is subjected to trauma they go into shock and their mind creates an amnesic barrier around the memory to forget the whole incident. The only problem is: this part of the mind thinks it is the whole and the child then grows up with schizophrenic tendencies.

This is a scientifically recognised phenomenon, but there is little we understand regarding what enters the small pocket in the mind when they are created. The people involved with helping these children have noted they become demonic and use foul language (they can't have heard before) when they access this area of the mind. This is quite compelling evidence for the existence of demons.

Do demons exist?

I know (from personal experience) there are spiritual angels so I see no reason why there can't be the existence of dark principalities that are mentioned in scripture. If I have encountered a demon – it has been through the tempting thoughts I have had while battling against my own struggle to walk with God. I have never actually seen a demon; so I'll leave that one for you to make up your own mind on. However, I would recommend you don't give them any credence whatsoever and the phrase: "In the name of Yeshua HaMashiach, I command all evil to depart from me," is quite a powerful phrase if you feel threatened.

It would be wiser for you to concentrate on walking upright before God and keep His commandments. Walking upright before God just means – treating everyone equally and keeping the commandments as meaningful principles you circumcise the heart with – to become a friend of God.

DIVINE LEGISLATION

First of all: I should mention here, the first time God said (in terms of divine legislation) anything about the Law was when He said: 'Do not partake of the forbidden fruit or you shall surely die.' This doesn't explain what He expects from His creation because the law seems to get more and more complicate (or drawn out) as the centuries unfold. The next time He mentions divine legislation was when He stated what's called the Royal Law.

The Royal Law:

1) Love God with all your heart and all your soul and all your strength.
2) Love your neighbour as yourself.

Then we received the **Ten Commandments**:

1) You shall have no other Gods before God.
2) Do not make any graven idols or bow down to them.
3) Do not take the lords name in vain (pretend to love God & sin deliberately).
4) Work six days, rest on the seventh and keep the Sabbath day holy.
5) Honour your mother and father.
6) Do not murder anyone.
7) Do not commit adultery.
8) Do not steal.
9) Do not lie.
10) Do not covet the things that belong to others,

After that, there was the Torah and it keeps getting more and more complicated (drawn out) right up to the time we received the Qur'ān. This may seem rather daunting – with the Kingdom Of God looming – it would be easy to believe the law is going to be impossible to know and keep because it seems to go on and on.

Here's the good news.

The only thing we need to do is keep the first utterance of law (not partaking of the fruit) to keep the Royal Law. Once we are able to honour this law (which is simple enough to keep in the heart) all the rest seem to fall away. For example: if I am upset by a neighbour for whatever reason I should remain calm and discuss my grievance in a civilised manner and not get angry. By doing this, I am honouring the Royal Law to love my neighbour as myself and I am also honouring all the other laws that have followed regarding anger.

Yeshua stated if you are angry with your neighbour you have broken the sixth commandment in the heart. God wants us to take these laws to heart.

This means that whenever you read the scriptural laws they should always support the simplified version spoken at the beginning (and glorify God – obviously). The more (longer) we – strive to – keep the Royal Law the easier it is to keep, just like an alcoholic will find it easier to stop drinking and not drink after they stop and endeavour to remain sober for a while. Science has confirmed it takes 38 days (of repeating something) to break a habit or create a habit. Sounds awfully similar to forty days and forty nights: I wonder if there is a connection.

THE LEGACY OF ISHMAEL

Scripture tells us an agreement was made between Sarai and her maidservant to let Abram father a child out of wedlock. This agreement was made because Sarai lacked the faith she would conceive a child of her own.

Both Sarai and Abram believed he would be the father of many nations, as God said, but God (at this time) had not revealed that Sarai would bare him a son. This lack of faith, lead to the birth of Ishmael the first born son of Abram and God said he would bless Ishmael and multiply him greatly, though his hand would be turned against every man and every man's hand would be turned against him.

Here we have a situation where God has openly admitted to creating unrest in the world and I think it's only fitting to address the reason why. I would like to make it clear I offer my blessings to these people without any prejudice toward their existence and I hope this booklet is well received by the entire world including all the descendants of Abraham.

I've often wondered how God might have felt about their lack of faith and I think it would be fair to say He would have been sympathetic because Sarai was, after all, old and she had been barren all her life.

I am aware that Abraham is known for his faith and he did indeed believe he would be the father of many nations (as God told him) but he did not believe Sarai, his wife, would be the mother of these nations. We know this because he lay with the Egyptian maidservant to conceive a child. I imagine if God had said you and Sarai will parent many nations, he would not have lay with the maidservant – and waited for Sarai's womb to be opened.

Anyway… their faith is not in question here because God did not make it clear what was going on, and I believe God wanted the situation that has arisen – in the world as a result of this agreement, today – for a reason. This highlights what happens when we take matters into our own hands and stray from the law. If Abram had kept the Royal Law (which Noah would have taught him in his formative years) he would have asked God continually until He told him what to do. This is the 64,000 dollar question. Would God have allowed a son to be born out of wedlock to make this powerful point – I am about to reveal?

I believe God would have told him to wait until Sarai's womb is opened and the opportunity to make the point, I am trying to highlight here, would have been lost – because God will not compromise his own law – ever.

Man (and woman): break the Royal Law – not God!
So what does it all mean, and what is this powerful point God wants us to know?

In the beginning God tried to explain, he is the one and only God and, how we should live – but it seemed his words fell on deaf ears.

Through the centuries God watched us (albeit with a deep sense of sadness because of our iniquitous behaviour) and found people who were willing to stand up for the truth. Just take a look at the people mentioned in scripture and it will become obvious they all have the same admirable traits God was (is) looking for in his creation. They all defied the established traditions; laid down by men who lust for power.

Abraham defied the tradition of worshiping many gods. Yeshua defied the tradition of observing the law literally in favour of keeping them in the heart and living by faith. These people were pleasing to God for they glorified him – and they did not lust for power. Abraham brought us two separate types of people that have secured the worshiping one god as an acceptable tradition which now out-numbers the nations that worship false gods.

Remember God declared to Abram he would multiply his descendants until they out-numbered the stars in the sky. I believe this was (is) an outstanding success.

So why did God allow (nigh create) a nation that is contentious by its nature? The answer here is simply: He wants us to realise – it is not enough to worship one God. We must also have a covenant with him too. Worshiping 'the' one God who has a covenant with his creation is what we need to establish everlasting peace.

After reading this booklet – I would like to think you have a clearer picture of what is expected of you, if you are to excel and become (as) one of the people God considers most pleasing. The kind of person who always stands up for what is right with a clear conscience and determination that glorifies the one God by not lusting for power at any level – be it temporal or spiritual.

THE TRUTH

CONTENTS

PART FIVE – HOW TO DISCERN THE TRUTH

PART SIX – THE EVIDENCE FOR TRUTH LIVES

PART SEVEN – THE TRUTH ABOUT THE KINGDOM

CAUSE AND EFFECT – PART EIGHT THAT IS OF THE SEVEN

PART FIVE
HOW TO DISCERN THE TRUTH

THE TRUTH ABOUT LIES

The way to know a truth, of any kind, is to know what a lie is. Once you ascertain something is a falsehood: the truth is revealed as an obvious corollary – usually with dire consequence if a belief system is hinged upon the foundation of a lie.

The irony of this (revelation) is – there is no such thing as a lie. This is because no lie can exist unless it is the twisted silhouette of the truth it seeks to undermine. This is why the saying goes: there's an element of truth in the lie. This does not mean a lie has any truth – because lies are a perversion of the truth. When the truth is twisted to create what is called a lie; it berates its own source to conceal the essence of the wisdom it originated from.

The whole of existence itself is based on the twisting motion of Pi and it can be found in everything from DNA helixes to seashells; from weather vortices to galaxies. It's as if twisting motion is what perpetuates reality. This means that twisting is innate and intrinsic to our existence but is it absolutely necessary to hide the truth.

NOTES

TWISTING SERVES A DUAL PURPOSE

1) The observation of twisting motion (fractals) reveals the physical world.
2) The understanding of twisting motion (lies) reveals the spiritual world.

Interesting (and beautiful) as fractals can be: we are primarily concerned with how the twisting of truth induces cause and effect on the spiritual and – all too often – the physical world.

How do we know the difference between the truth and a lie?

Once you recognize a falsehood is a twisted form of some truth, you have the means to know the difference between 'the truth' and 'the lie'. The only problem is 'the truth' is the hardest thing to accept because the saying also goes 'the truth hurts'. However, this is inaccurate because a person that believes (knows) the truth in the first place can *never* be hurt. People can only be hurt, by the truth, if they originally believed a lie (twisted truth) to be true in some way. It takes courage to see truth – or indeed observe it.

So the lie does not exist and all we have is truth(s) or twisted forms of truth(s). This, flawless fact, is a difficult thing to take onboard but – unfortunately – you may be able to run (cast this book aside) but you cannot hide (escape the tribulations that will soon beset the world).

The '*Truth*' was established thousands of years before you were here and it will endure forever after you have gone. Take heed because it does have the power – as scripture declares – to separate the marrow from the bone. By the time you finish this book you will understand the full power (implications) of the *Truth* and the dire need to seek it wherever and whenever you can. The good news is: this book will not only reveal the means to discern the *Truth* but it will assist you in finding the courage to accept it without fear of the hurt normally associated with discovering truth.

An example of this can be seen with the colour of snow. Snow is white – correct? This is *only* true if snow really is white. When we look at snow under a microscope we see it is a crystal which forms under specific conditions to be clear as glass. The reason why snow appears to be white is because the light is reflected off the edges of each crystal thus we don't actually see the colour of white but the extreme diffusion of light.

If you were debating the colour of snow and you convinced everyone it was white you would, without realising, be perpetuating a lie or – non-truth to be more precise. With time you would have a large following of people who believe what you said and thus you and your believers are all in danger of being hurt when the truth is revealed.

This is because the ego can only accept slight adjustments as it becomes more and more informed of the truth and less and less inclined to believe assumption.

In this booklet, you are less likely to feel this effect because you can take some time to deal with the truth before admitting to the world you thought otherwise: indeed some (if not most) will pretend they either knew the true answer anyway or say it was not something they had given much thought about – thus avoiding looking stupid in front of others.

However, in a group environment it is not nice to be made out to be a fool – which just goes to show it is wiser to say nothing than to remove all doubt of ignorance.

NOTES

WE NEED AN ANCHOR!

Some might say: 'The *Truth* is an anchor' and to some extent this is accurate. But we are embarking on a quest to discover the *Truth* so we need to find something that will not change under any kind of stress *(whether spiritual or physical)* to recover the *Truth* that has been twisted through the centuries.

PHILOSOPHY?

A philosophical viewpoint might be a good starting-point – to begin our pursuit of *Truth*. A secure idea devised by man that has been able to withstand the rigour and pace of change in the modern world might provide a good launching pad. A philosopher (with a subjective viewpoint) can claim to have 'the *Truth*' and the way they give account of the world, they observe, is the only means by which we can gauge the accuracy of their claim. If we refer to the objective observation based on the fact *Truth* is something that exists without any form of twisting, we can place any philosophical idea under due-stress to test the veracity of its source.

Many philosophical ideas have surfaced throughout the centuries but none have remained in a position of dominance for long. This is because a new idea comes along and the next philosophical era takes shape. For this reason, it is unlikely that any single individual can be in possession of the whole (perfect) *Truth*.

SCIENCE?

Einstein used light as a constant to base his theories on; and recent discoveries have shown that light is able to slow down or speed up. One would have thought the red-shift phenomena would have given this basic fact away, many years ago. So the speed of light along with gravity can be ruled out as a constant because we know they are subject to change.

Science today is observing atoms that disappear then reappear before their very eyes. They have sought to create a basis for understanding this strange phenomena with something they have called quantum mechanics. This area of science basically does little more than acknowledge the fact that 'some things are beyond explanation' as they attempt to equate probability. Or to put it in simple terms – they are guessing it, because they don't know what is going on. Since quantum mechanics was introduced; the scientific community has gone on a free-for-all with their imagination and they have devised ever greater theories that cannot be disproved.

Science deserves less credibility than religion because it professes to be the conclusion of observable facts when it has actually entered the realm of faith with theories that are beyond reproach. Theories are subject to change and are therefore a formless foundation (of sand) for securing the understanding of truth.

At least the religions are honest, and decent, enough to admit faith is a prerequisite for seeking wisdom. Some of the theories scientists have postulated sound fascinating, but they have no practical use – even if they are accurate – unless you plan to use a black-hole to percolate time or something.

Those who choose to stand by science should take heed the discipline has a strange habit of stabbing its patrons in the back. The single cell, for example, is anything but simple. In fact – the single cell amoeba has a means of propulsion called the Flagellum Motor that puts anything that man has made to shame. If evolution is to be believed then the amoeba is more advanced than Star-Trek and man; at worst is going in reverse in terms of improving himself to survive and; at best still trying to catch up with the amoeba.

For this 'good' reason: science is to be ruled out before we even start our pursuit of the *Truth* because science has set itself up for a fall right from the beginning when it embraced the concept of logic which is basically – the one plus one is three that gives answers it cannot see. For example: sweat is water (1) skin is solid (plus 1) water cannot pass through solid surfaces unless it has holes (equals 3).

Some might claim proudly that science has brought us so far we can land a man on the moon within a fraction of a second accuracy. To which I say: 'And yet they cannot cure the common cold.' I do not wish to berate science because it has actually achieved so much, but it has entered the realm of faith and there are other disciplines that are more expertise (even an authority) on this subject.

Science itself is also subject to change. The Theory of Relativity has been proven correct – yet it has not been granted the status of law because it violates the Law of Gravity. The fact the scientific community does not know how to legitimize a theory that has been proven correct proves science has 'lost the plot' and we are forced to seek truth elsewhere.

RELIGION?

There are a multitude of religions that claim to possess the *Truth* – some that have been founded by a single person who have professed to have the whole (perfect) *Truth* while others have been the culmination of many people's work (science) and sometimes centuries of tradition. We will examine all these with reference to the means we have to discern 'the *Truth*' without reservation for the pursuit of ascertaining the whole (perfect) *Truth*.

There are only two things we can use as an anchor, other than the *Truth* itself, to discover the whole perfect *Truth* – and that is:

1) The accurate fulfilment of prophecy (prophecies).
2) The clean – pure – fruits of those who profess to have the *Truth*.

It's unlikely that anyone has clean – pure – fruits so all the televised evangelists can also be ruled out and it should be noted: the author of this book does not profess to have the whole (perfect) *Truth* because the *Truth* is something that is followed once it is discovered and it leads to ever deeper levels of understanding and wisdom which facilitates a greater respect and love for: *Truth*(s)!

You (the reader) are encouraged to discover the *Truth* for yourself. I (the author) will give you the tools to find it and observe it as you follow it to a place of wisdom that knows no boundaries.

So we are left with 'accurate fulfilment of prophecy' as a starting point.

If the fulfilment of prophecy – found in scripture – is observable and accurate: the other accounts given in scripture are given legitimate credibility with which we can begin our pursuit of the *Truth*.

This then means that discerning the *Truth* will facilitate happiness and prosperity as you protect yourself from the temptations of the evil that surrounds us today. The question remains: Which religion? This in itself has been one of the most difficult questions to answer in modern times.

PART SIX
THE EVIDENCE FOR TRUTH LIVES

THE POWER OF PROPHECY

If we read scripture and know how to interpret the prophecies contained within them, we immediately see that the events which are unfolding before our very eyes are echoes in the words written thousands of years ago. What is strange is: the people who wrote the prophecies had no idea what they meant. They were required to write them (regardless of their unawareness of their meaning) for the later generations to understand and act upon.

The reason why this was charged is the very same reason why you (the reader) are reading this book. It's as if God knew people would need something, like an anchor, to seek the truth in the later days – so He (God) revealed the future to a small group of people, he trusted, to let us have something to cross-reference and check to verify the authenticity of the scripture He prepared for us.

So the prophecies written in scripture have been written with the express intention of establishing the other parts of scripture are a credible source of information pertaining to the *Truth*. It is ironic that we seem to have met each other half-way in this manner. We (reader and author) are seeking an anchor and He (God) having deliberately prepared that very thing for us; in anticipation of our needs.

The prophecies also serve to assist people in understanding the sequence of events for (His) people to take heart He has our best interests in mind; as the tribulations get worse and worse toward the end.

NOTES
_____
_____
_____
_____
_____
_____
_____
_____
_____
_____

THE SURVIVAL OF RELIGION

The main religions that have survived to this day include:

PAGANISM

There are remnants of these still around but none of them provide any credible prophetic writings that we may examine to scrutinise with due-diligence against our own prescribed test-facility – to ascertain truth.

HINDUISM

They are still waiting for their idols, that show no signs of life, to animate after several centuries – and it doesn't look like they are about to start making any interesting moves any time soon. It's not quite clear if these people have anything prophetic to say because their idols are (well) for the lack of a better word – idle on the subject. Perhaps we should say their false idols give false ideas because they are (by definition) idle and without life.

If you believe in many gods and something goes wrong in life you will naturally think the god(s) of whatever or whoever was angry with the god(s) you worship …and you will be more inclined to not accept responsibility when things do go wrong.

BUDDHISM AND SPIRITUALITY

These are in their basic elements so similar they can be addressed together as ways of life (not wholly religions) that have no prophetic writings at all. Thus they have no means to verify their claim to legitimacy in any way other than the pursuit of illusions of signs from the perspective of paranormal incitements.

For example they claim we return by way of reincarnation then attempt to formulate pseudo-scientific evidence for this by sending people into deep regression – when the truth is no one has ever returned from the dead other than one person – and he does not advocate Buddhism or Spirituality. If you believe in no god(s) and something goes wrong in your life you will naturally think life is not meant to be enjoyed because nature is unforgiving or people are unenlightened.

Thinking nature is unforgiving is a somewhat depressing and negative approach to life and thinking people that are unenlightened are at fault places them beneath enlightened people. In this kind of environment where one person is above another there is no-room for love to flourish.

<u>MONOTHEISM</u>

Monotheism – or the worship of a single God – was established by a man named Abraham and while the idea of monotheism was a little known idea in ancient times – Abraham was the first to make a stand against the worship of idols and this act of defying the tradition of worshiping many gods was endorsed by God when He introduced Himself to Abraham to establish a covenant with him and his descendants. The God that spoke to Abraham told him He would make his descendants number more than the stars in the sky.

Thus he became the patriarch of three major religious faiths: Judah – Islam – Christianity (the Lost Ten Tribes of Israel) and it can be seen the promise God made has come true because there are a lot of people who have come from Abraham.

Furthermore – we can see the religions of these faiths have prophecies that we can use to verify their authenticity to make an informed decision. Belief in one God also means that is something goes wrong in your life you will naturally look inward: because it means you know you have done something wrong.

I am tempted to simply leave the answer as 'One' without giving any credence to the other religions who seek to endorse multiple deities. However, I shall give account of multiple deity based religions – cultures – traditions – nations etc. and how they have failed to prosper.

Egypt – Fallen – Never To Know Supremacy Again.
Babylon – First Fallen Empire – Gold
Maya – Fallen.
Persia – Second Fallen Empire – Silver
Aztec – Fallen.
Greece – Third Fallen Empire – Bronze
Rome – Fourth Fallen Empire – Iron
China – Gentiles Time To Come To Fulfilment.
Russia – King of the Gogs (North) To Attack the Apple of His Eye (Israel).
Europe – Fifth (and Final) Empire about to fall – Iron and Clay

The gods of all the cultures – nations – empires listed above have failed to make their ways prosper. Europe – China and Russia are prophecies yet (soon) to be fulfilled. The prophecies surrounding these countries and empires will be examined later to verify credibility.

NOTES

THE EVE OF ETERNITY

The final book in scripture The Revelation of Jesus Christ gives us a chronological sequence of events that culminate toward the full realisation of the Kingdom of God. The prophetic writings found in this book run parallel to all the prophetic writing of the prophets in the Old Testament and thus we can depict its meaning from the way it self-interprets it own symbols. The vision seen by John describes a scroll that was retrieved by the Lamb of God Jesus and he describes what happens in the world as each of the seven seals on the scroll is broken.

Seal 1 – False prophets will deceive the multitude.
Seal 2 – There will be wars (and Yeshua spoke of rumours of wars)
Seal 3 – Famine will grip many nations.
Seal 4 – Pestilence (death) will become widespread.
Seal 5 – Tribulation (earthquakes and tsunamis) and Martyrdom shake the world.
Seal 6 – Heavenly signs. It will appear like the stars are falling from the sky.
------------ a period of silence in heaven while the saints are being sealed.
Seal 7 – Plagues will fall upon the world.

It would be easy to see how we have already had the first five seals because we have had false prophets, wars, famine, pestilence and tribulations including martyrdom; and while non-believers may argue these are all natural phenomena – or the things that constitute famine and pestilence, for example, cannot be counted as scriptural prophecy coming to pass – they are intensifying.

We could infer the meteor that fell near Tunguska that destroyed miles of forestry could be seen as a heavenly sign, but it may be more accurate to remain true to the scriptural reference of a third of the stars falling from heaven which is generally accepted (among theologians) to mean angels being cast out of heaven.

Therefore we can expect to see a pronounced level of falling stars (meteors) that are unusually more intense than the normal showers we experience each year. The chances are this will occur in September when we expect to see showers but the scientists will reason the higher intensity of meteors to some arbitrary force of nature rather than acknowledge the prophetic writings of scripture.

There is then a period of silence in heaven while the saints are being sealed and this will begin in earnest when people will have been reported to have simply vanished into thin air. The churches had called this the rapture and tried to twist its meaning to give the impression; those who are not taken are left to suffer eternal damnation. However, the truth is this gathering of the saints and it is simply a powerful sign the days are now numbered from this moment. This is the moment the little flock will be taken to a safe place to be instructed on how to assist the Lord (Yeshua HaMashiach) when he returns to establish the Kingdom of God.

This will take place during the Day of the Lord while the Saints are 'being sealed' and the world experiences ever greater tribulations including: a third of the vegetation will burn up; a third of the seas will turn to blood; a third of the waters will turn bitter; a third of the sun, moon and stars will not shine and a great military force will rise to power and gather. Then the seven plagues will begin when the two witnesses will appear in Jerusalem to proclaim The Kingdom of God.

These seven plagues are designed to bring people to humility in the same way Moses was trying to bring Pharaoh to release the nation of Israel. This will be because the people who are disobedient and haughty will still refuse to believe the Kingdom of God is drawing near even though all the signs have been and gone. The duration of the seven plagues is: three and a third years leading up to the slaying of the two witnesses in the streets of Jerusalem. The witnesses will lay in the streets for thee and a third days – then they will rise up and join the Lord (Yeshua the Christ) who will be arriving with all the angels of heaven and His Saints to establish the Kingdom of God.

The question is: if you are a non-believer – at which point will you decide there is more than mere quackery going on here. Will you decide the wars and famine and pestilence is proof enough; or will the heavenly signs be enough; or will the strange disappearance of people is enough; or the devastation that befalls the world with burning vegetation or seas of blood is enough; or the seven plagues are enough.

You may be a believer (in which case Jesus has instructed you to not be dismayed by all the troubles you see about you) or you may become a believer later – but what is incredible is the fact people will still defy God even when Christ is descending from heaven with all His angels and Saints.

One final point here that may be important is to bear in mind the fact scripture states the only reason why God sent His Son back was to save the world from total annihilation.

NOTES

CLARIFYING THE TRUTH – THROUGH THE LAW

Let us clarify the law that there is no confusion as to what its purpose is.

As I read through Genesis I get this overwhelming feeling the book is not about creation but rather it is about the introduction of law. I have this feeling because the text does not focus on the intricate way God created everything. In fact – I get the impression this whole process of creation has been gleaned over to give an overview with particular detail given to the way people behave. As I read through scripture this seems to be a theme that continually has importance so it is with deliberation I will give an account of what is going on here and why.

<u>THE ROYAL LAW</u>

People have asked me what the most important temptation Yeshua the Christ refused when he was in the wilderness. The obvious answer they expect is the final one when he refused to bow down to the Devil but I explain it is the first: because refusing to turn stone to bread he was refusing to bow to the Devil then and He also showed He didn't need to prove He was the Messiah at the same time.

The fact Jesus was able to resist the temptation to turn stone to bread after being without food for 40 days and 40 nights was an awesome achievement; and this alone proves he is worthy to be King of Kings as prophesised in the scriptures. He led a life that was pleasing to God and he never defiled his body – so he became the perfect sacrifice at Passover to complete his ministry. So if he had the ability to resist the temptation to turn stone to bread when he was extremely hungry - why did he turn the water to wine when he said he was not ready to do so? When he said: 'My time has not yet come.' He wasn't saying: 'I don't have the power'.

We know this because he used the power and it happened. He was saying that turning water to wine was hardly the right way to use the power he had. This may be because he was still waxing in the spirit or perhaps there was another reason; but we cannot ignore the fact he said his time had not yet come. He made this confession himself and it served him well - I might add – because we can look at the situation and ask ourselves why did he do this when he was strong enough to resist extreme hunger? You'd think he could easily have said: 'No I won't do it – because I'm not ready.' But he didn't say that – instead he performed his first miracle and as such he abused the power he had.

So: why did he do it?

Theologians say the turning of water to wine was symbolic of the new covenant he would establish later on but I wonder why he would use symbolism when he was here to clarify things. Using such symbolism would make it more difficult for us to understand scripture – not easier. Perhaps it was symbolic but I believe there was a more practical reason...

The answer is simple: Jesus understood the profound meaning of the *Royal Law* and this act would give us (his people) the insight we need to follow his example.

THE ROYAL LAW IS:

1)   Love God with all your heart and all your strength and all your soul and...
2)   Love your neighbour as yourself.

The second part is so easy to understand - a child could get it. The first part (however) is rather tricky; and as such we have seen countless wars between nations that profess to know the answer. Even unto this present day people strike out with what they think is the correct way to worship God and they are all – too often – ready to kill for that they believe.

The, turning of water into wine, incident provides an answer for the entire world to see how we should keep the Royal Law. Resisting temptation to acquire something you want (for yourself) more than anything else is how you keep the Royal Law. This also confirms the requirement to offer ourselves up as a sacrifice because it is sacrifice that allows us to empathise with God who lost his perfect creation to the disobedience of mankind in the beginning.

This may give us a hint but it certainly does not answer why Jesus turned the water to wine. He turned the water to wine because he was using his power for someone else and not himself (and although he was not ready) this simple act proved that looking after people is more important than pious rituals or prayer – while we are here, on earth, at least.

This, then, means – as Jesus obviously knew – that by loving your neighbour as yourself you are also (at the same time) demonstrating your love for God. So anyone who says: "I put God before anyone and everything" is twisting the Royal Law to their own end and they are hiding behind the words they find in scripture to try and support their own obscured belief. All too often these people continually seek to exalt themselves and they should beware the *Truth* will reveal their shame if they do not change their ways and humble themselves accordingly.

When Jesus said: 'Unless a man forsakes everyone even his mother and father is not worthy of me,' he was not saying: 'It's ok to disregard the Royal Law.' To follow Christ is to love everyone equally and it is possible to forsake family to love others equally without making your family suffer. If anyone suffers by the action of your hand, family or otherwise, you have failed to keep the Royal Law.

This is the law that Yeshua HaMashiach said he had come to fulfil and everyone should strive to emulate that wonderful task.

NOTES

WHAT DOES GRACE MEAN?

The common perception of grace is one where the law is subject to generalization – that a person who lives in grace need not concern themselves with the finer detail of the commandments of God because the blood of Christ washes away all sin and thus the follower of Christ is no longer under the law.

The follower of Christ repents daily and takes measure to do all they can to emulate the Lamb of God (Yeshua the Christ). They then engage in learning the ways of Christ to ensure they follow him in reflective harmony to the character they perceive.

However, grace has greater meaning which can only be clarified when we observe the way devil worshipers view their leader satan. They perceive Lucifer as a liberator who gave mankind freedom where as Yeshua is perceived as an oppressor who gave mankind laws. This situation is a reflection of the Garden of Eden incident: where man was told not to partake of the forbidden fruit by God or else he would surely die but he was informed by the serpent he would surely not die if he did partake of the forbidden fruit.

The sense of irony that things have not changed since the beginning of mans time on earth is enough to conclude there has to be a truth lurking somewhere in this situation. Eat the forbidden fruit and become free to think for ourselves (without God) or do not eat the forbidden fruit and retain obedience to the law (with God providing guidance).

This then indicates the option is – freedom or slavery – and it is easy to see (at first hand) how this is the case when we consider the doctrines of the church that speak of eternal hell and damnation for those who do not capitulate to the decrees of the priesthood. These church beliefs are all false doctrine that have been deliberately put in place to instil the kind of fear that ensures the masses are enslaved while the worship of satan has emphasised the rights of individuals to have the freedom to engage in any immoral actions so long as they can stay out of trouble with the laws man has established.

In short – the Ten Commandments are abhorred by anyone who does not want to live a life of virtue before the Lord and they find ways to reason away their decision to continue their life of revelry by pointing the finger and blaming God for anything they see is wrong.

They blame God for death – they blame God for violence – they blame God for the religions that enslave people – they blame God for everything and this is all prophesied in scripture that says: there will be a multitude of false accusers in the end days. The word satan means false accuser so the people who point their fingers and lay blame are so like the Devil they do not know the severity of their failure to understand the reason for creation.

They lack the alacrity required for soul searching and thus they have no soul.

Grace was established in order to provide the same situation in the Garden of Eden when God left Adam and Eve alone in the garden to see if they would or would not obey His commandment. Believing the blood of Christ washes our sins daily is fine: but that does not mean we are not expected to keep the commandments. That is 'the' truth – we are still free to choose which path we walk. A life of obedience to God where He guides us to eternal joy: or a life of disobedience to God where we are free to do as we please. Either way – the law that was first uttered regarding the fruit still stands. If we choose disobedience we choose death (which is easy to believe is going to happen regardless of behaviour) or if we choose obedience we choose life eternal because God knows He can trust us to enter His Kingdom. John wrote in the Revelation of Jesus Christ he heard the angels say the words: 'Who is worthy?'

I say: 'Indeed...! Who is worthy?'

Until man finds a cure for disease and death, this truth regarding the forbidden fruit (sin) will prevail forever and given the fact we could die tomorrow, this surely means the Kingdom of God is truly at hand.

NOTES

WHAT DOES 'GLORY OF GOD' MEAN?

The word glory is described in the Oxford dictionary as:

glo·ry (glôr 'ē, gl ōr 'ē)

n. pl. **glo·ries**

1. Great honour, praise, or distinction accorded by common consent; renown.
2. Something conferring honour or renown.
3. A highly praiseworthy asset: *Your wit is your crowning glory.*
4. Adoration, praise, and thanksgiving offered in worship.
5. Majestic beauty and splendour; resplendence: *The sun set in a blaze of glory.*
6. The splendour and bliss of heaven; perfect happiness.
7. A height of achievement, enjoyment, or prosperity: *ancient Rome in its glory.*
8. A halo, nimbus, or aureole. Also called *gloriole.*

intr.v. **glo·ried, glo·ry·ing, glo·ries**

To rejoice triumphantly; exult: *a sports team that gloried in its hard-won victory*

The means by which men obtain glory is generally perceived as winning in battle – thus if we are to assume this is the same for God we have to ask ourselves what or where is the battle. In the Torah (first five books of the Old Testament) Moses asks the Lord God to show him his glory and God introduced him to the Lamb of God – Yeshua HaMashiach. This means the way a person lives their life in humility and complete selflessness to love others with equal measure is the way God is glorified.

In other words the battle is within and not in the world – to cleanse the soul and wax strong enough in the spirit to enter the Kingdom of God. The blood of Christ cleanses the soul but it is up to us individually to grow in faith to wax strong in the spirit.

The way a person lives (according to the commandments) glorifies God and thus the name of God is revealed in the way they love others to fulfil the Royal Law. The Hallowed Name of God cannot be uttered – because it can only be perceived in the Son as He glorifies God.

This, then, means the fullness of God's Glory will only be fully realised when the creation is complete and Yeshua (the King of Kings) hands over the key to the Kingdom to His Father and the physical creation (known universe) is conflagrated in a flash with all the iniquitous children who refused to accept the Father as their true sovereign Lord (spiritual parent). This means that whenever someone humbles themselves of their own free-will to display love for others they glorify God because God is within them in that moment.

The plan from the beginning of the creation is to bring: everyone to become as one with the One who is in all. Thus: 'I Am That I Am' may become, 'All That Is One (In) All: As One.'

This is the Hallowed Name (Glory) of God – which can only be observed.

NOTES

PART SEVEN
THE TRUTH ABOUT THE KINGDOM

THE SEARCH OF THE SOUL FOR: FAITH

The question of faith is often asked by those who feel trumped by the notion they are unable to discuss the concept of something that by its definition means: a belief of something that does not need proof or evidence to exist.

The question is normally asked by those who do not believe there is a God (atheists) because those who believe there is a God (theists) stipulate they need no proof there is a God – because everything they see is proof enough.

Understandably – this can be frustrating if not infuriating because it leaves the non-believer unable to combat the whole concept of the existence of a God and they frequently resort to levity saying evidence (logic) is paramount – even though they do not fully appreciate they have their own faith – while the believer maintains their assertion there is no need for evidence.

Here is a 'Home Truth' on that issue:

A theist professes to believe in the existence of a God and they have faith in the promises made by their God to deliver the Kingdom of God. That's the same as saying – the Lord will establish: a world where everyone is free, happy and equal – not to mention immortal. An atheist professes to believe there is no God and they have faith in the in the science of mankind to sort out all the current problems in the world – including the quest for immortality.

This then means both the atheist and the theist have a belief and both have a faith in something – the difference being the theist believes in God whereas the atheist believes in Man. Thus to find a faith we need only look at the way things are in the world to make an informed decision as to which of the two has the best chance of success. This is where things get interesting because a lot will depend on the individual's ability to assess the things they see (not to mention the way they see things) and their ability to take a calculated risk based on the information they have available to them.

Given the possibility many (deliberate) lies have been thrown into the intelligence of the information available to cause confusion – we must also find a way to determine what is true and what is untrue.

So – because both (atheists and theists) have faith the choice is simple:

Faith – God – Promise – Kingdom
Faith – Man – Science – Utopia

Now that we have dispensed with the vanity of attacking faith and found the determining factor for belief is faith in either man or God we can now turn our attention to the means by which we develop our faith in either of these directions and it is good to know we can focus on either until we decide which we want to stick to.

At this time – the individual will no longer need to question someone else's faith because they have taken the time and effort with courage and determination to make their decision.

Furthermore – there is the issue of standing your ground.

If you believe man has the ability to succeed and you place your faith in mankind, you are violating every single principle of scripture if you use scripture to support your stance because true equality is the means by which we glorify God.

An example of this may include making remarks such as 'The meek will inherit the earth.' It is true – the meek will inherit the earth – but how can anyone be meek in a world where hierarchy and power structures are present. The basic truth here is – are you willing to be meek and not assume or attain any power over others or do you want to have the opportunity to hanker for power?

If you are not willing to be humble, unassuming, meek, or at least learn how to attain these qualities you are placing your faith in man to use science to establish utopia and you are advocating all the problems that are in the world today.

Even if you think religion is to blame you have been misled to believe in the 'us and them' scenario to develop a prejudice against what you think is a false belief. Any religion that has a power structure is not of God – it is of man and thus it is easy to get lost in all the confusion which seems to beset the whole world today.

You – are a part of this world and the choice is simple – do you want hierarchy or equality. These are the polarized differences: and mankind stands on one side and God stands on the other.

THE ILLUSION: FREEDOM VERSES SLAVERY

Even the Masonic Order (who is setting up this utopian world of hierarchy – pyramid of power under the guise of two brotherhoods The Illuminati and The Luminari) believe there were two Sons of Light: satan and Yeshua.

Of course the truth is Yeshua is 'of the light' whereas satan is the light-bearer.

As previously mentioned, satan is seen as the one who gave mankind freedom and liberty and Yeshua the Christ (Jesus) is seen as the one who enslaved us with laws – but you have to ask yourself to be realistic – if we are all free to do as we please there would be chaos (as we see in the world today) because there would be no one and nothing to stop anyone from doing whatever they want.

If you are thinking: 'Ah... but we have the police to stop people doing whatever they want.' I would have to reply: 'Hello... they enforce law. Man's law that facilitates hierarchy and power.'

Hierarchy facilitates lust for power. Power that is usurped can only be attained if you step on other people. If you are stepping on people – where is the love?

Think of the Kingdom of God like the road and you are the vehicle. You have the freedom to go wherever you want but you have to drive carefully and safely (which is what the laws ensure) to reach your destination in one piece and without hurting yourself or others. While Yeshua may be the one with the laws – you don't get caught up in the laws once you learn how to live within them (just like you don't worry too much about them when you drive) and that is then you experience this immense feeling of 'true' freedom and liberty – because we are all as one with God as His sons (and daughters).

What do you want: chaos or harmony – hierarchy or equality – love or fear?

MAN IS CHAOS – HIERARCHY – FEAR (AND) GOD IS HARMONY – EQUALITY – LOVE.

WHAT IS TRUTH?

Pilate said to him. "What is truth?" and when he had said this, he went outside again to the Jews and said to them, "I find no fault in Him at all". John 18:38

It was more likely Pilate didn't even want an answer. However let us consider the way such a conversation might ensue between a theist (who knows the truth); and an atheist (who knows science).

Atheist: In the immortal words of Pilate: 'What is truth?'

Theist: Truth is a concrete noun - not an abstract noun.

Atheist: The common-sense notion that truth is a kind of 'correspondence with the facts' has never been worked out to anyone's satisfaction. Therefore, we have 'Minimal Theory' to discern truth using 'pure' logic.

Theist: If 'pure' logic had any intrinsic value we would know the observations of science are facts and thus they would not be presented as theories.

Atheist: Logic is the process by which we reveal that which cannot be seen because it provides us with facts which are observable using repeatable experiments that verify the validity of such findings.

Theist: What has science determined exactly?

Atheist: 'Theoretically' we know the nature of this reality is co-dependent on another reality that operates outside our own laws of nature and vice versa.

Theist: If science is aware there is another reality, that cannot be observed using repeatable experiments that verify the validity of findings, how can science be sure of anything (ever)?

Atheist: Theories are proof of the findings science makes.

Theist: If this is true why are they debated?

Atheist: OK... What is truth?

Theist: Truth is a concrete noun - not an abstract noun. Science shows that all of reality bows to the illusion of life and death, thus nothing is real but the way one person treats another person. Therefore truth is personified within a person who is in a state of 'knowing' the way to eternal life.

This is to say: truth is a concrete noun, such as Jesus Christ or anyone who is in Christ and keeps the commandments, not an abstract noun, such as a philosophical idea that can be explained in logical terms - pure or otherwise.

These seven points are scientific observation of reality.

1. Quanta particles operate outside our realm of natural laws.

2. Time ceases to exist at the smallest (quantum) of levels.

3. Everything at its smallest level seems to recede into nothingness - yet nothingness makes up all that exists.

4. Light or electro-magnetic energy, is what holds all quanta particles together - thus all matter is held together by (and is made of) light.

5. Our world and all matter is made up of "invisible" particles.

6. There appear to be parallel realities - the Quanta World and The Natural World - both operating with their own set of laws yet one depends entirely upon the other for its existence.

7. There appears to be an 'eternal' inter-connectedness between all elements. The 'Entanglement Theory'.

Now that we have established truth is a concrete noun and not an abstract noun; we can move on to understanding the state of 'knowing' that leads to eternal life. Recent surveys have shown that crime levels and health levels, including mortality rates and even levels of happiness are directly proportionate to the equality a society has.

This is a red flag that proves all of scripture is true. Immediately after Adam and Eve partook of the forbidden fruit God said in Genesis 3:16: To the woman he said, "I will surely multiply your pain in childbirth; in pain you shall bring forth children. Your desire shall be for your husband, and he shall rule over you."Let us be clear about what happened here.

God was telling the woman He would punish her with childbirth pain but the last part He tells her the consequences of having partaken of the forbidden fruit.

God was not saying He would make her subject to the man, He was saying this is the result of sin entering the world. This means satan had used the innocence of the woman to introduce his ways which counter God's ways - thus the power structure that God said was set in place was also the introduction of the image of the Beast.

All of scripture testifies to the equality of one and all: that this is what God wants for all mankind and Jesus Christ showed us how we should live in this fashion. The life He lived showed how a person should take care to never raise their head above another - and we should reject the image of the Beast (power structure) by not lusting for authority. In other words... followers should recognize what causes a person to lust for authority, is the breaking of the commandments, so they can take measures to avoid defiling themselves.

Every word in scripture testifies to this because even when God says, "I shall appoint a king" we can see, if we read this in context, God has been forced by the people of Israel to do this against His wishes - which is why He goes on to tell them the problems that will ensue because they have introduced a king. Furthermore, there are the laws that state how the king is to act as a subject to the people which seems to have been mysteriously removed from canonized scripture.

It is not possible to quote all of scripture here, so I shall draw on one that is a potent example of the simplicity of this truth I have outlined: But Jesus called them to Him and said, "You know that the rulers of the Gentiles lord it over them, and their great ones exercise authority over them. It shall not be so among you. But whoever would be great among you must be your servant." Matthew 20:25-26

We are now edging ever closer to understanding the state of 'knowing' the way to eternal life, I previously mentioned, and the truth can thus (so far) be shown as:

Hierarchy is the image of the Beast and to lust for authority is accepting The Mark of the Beast – whereas equality is the image of God and to avoid lusting for authority is to receive The Mark of God.

Jesus then shows us how we are all as one in God through Him with: "I do not ask for these only, but also for those who will believe in me that they may all be one, just as you, Father, are in me, and I in you, that they also may be in us, so that the world may believe that you sent me." John 17:20-21

This concludes the understanding of: What is truth... because we can now see - a person (who is a concrete noun named Jesus the Saviour - *Yeshua HaMashiach*) has requested God and all who read this to recognize those who keep the laws - and treat each other with equality - and accept the living Christ is the Truth the Way and the Light means a person can find a way to eternal life. Faith in God through Christ is the state of 'knowing' which brings peace of mind.

As a believer strives to overcome the temptations of the adversary (satan) the Glory of God becomes apparent because equality is the image of God and those (who are in Christ) become the embodiment of Truth which is the (unpronounceable) Hallowed Name of God.

NOTES

(IN) THE NAME OF GOD

The God of the monotheistic religions has been given various names throughout the centuries. All of which have been words that describe God in some way. For example: Hashem is the Hebrew word that means 'the Name'; Allah is the Arabic word that means 'The God'. The list goes on and on, needless to say anyone can look into these descriptive names and find a fascinating subject that will invariably offer an insight into the minds of those who have developed a love for their creator.

For centuries, Israel considered it sacrilege to utter the Name of God; and even now, there are many who consider it wrong to pronounce the name without proper reverence. In these modern times, people are becoming more and more at ease with using the Name YHWH (pronounced - Youd Hey vWah Hey or Yahweh for short) which translates to - Hand Behold Nail Behold because the Name Yahweh is considered a reflection of the Name Yeshuah, (or Yea'shuah) which is the Name of Jesus Christ.

This is because scripture tells us the Messiah will reveal the Hallowed Name of God but the name YHWH is pronounceable and not ineffable, so there may be more to the picture than meets the eye.

This article will show exactly how Jesus has revealed the ineffable Name of God.

During a murder trial, the prosecution makes a point of using the name of the victim as often as possible. The reason why is because they know, the more times they utter a name of the victim, the more the jury will perceive them as a real person; and they can then use the natural compassion people have toward a real person to support their conclusions.

From this, we can understand the reason why scripture tells us to avoid uttering the names of false gods is because the uttering of their names makes them more real. This also explains why the various faiths consider it inappropriate to use the Name of God without propriety of heart, mind and soul.

Scripture tells us God sent the Word to reveal His Hallowed ineffable Name, even though we already have the descriptive name known to be (YHWH) Yahweh Elohim. This may seem puzzling especially as we are told Jesus will utter then Name of God when He returns; and the wicked will be destroyed at the hearing of this Name. It's as if we are told: on the one hand, you can know the Name of God but, on the other hand, only Christ will be able to utter it when He returns.

Given the fact scripture tells us God is not the author of confusion it would be fair to ask ourselves:

1) Why did God send the Word to reveal His Hallowed Name when we already know the descriptive Name is Yahweh Elohim, and only Jesus will be able to utter the actual Hallowed Name?

2) What is the Hallowed ineffable Name of God?

3) Does the fact God sent the Word mean we can use the Name with more regularity now, to make God become more real in our hearts and minds, even though the uttering of His Name has been banned for centuries?

The answers to these questions can be found in scripture.

Let us start at the beginning where Genesis 1:26 says: "Let us make man in our image". The first thing we need to do is verify each of these words to be sure of what is being said. It turns out that the word 'make' more predominantly means 'advance', thus we can accurately re-phrase the verse to say: "Let us advance man in our image'. This has a profound effect on the whole understanding of scripture now, because we can suddenly see everything written, in scripture, is designed to advance us in some way.

When we look to the verse that says God will send His Word to reveal His Hallowed Name it doesn't take much to realise there is a profound link at an intrinsic level between the advancement of man and the revealing of the ineffable Hallowed Name of God.

This gives us an idea why God sent His Word; that we may be advanced in some way. Having this in mind, we can begin to understand the Hallowed Name of God can be revealed in that which we are advanced to.

Revelation 22:4 - And they will see His face and His name on their foreheads. Micah 6:9 - The Lord's voice cries to the city wisdom shall see Your Name hear the rod who has appointed it.

These verses tell us the Name of God is something that is visible as well as something that is pronounceable. If we look back to the beginning again, in **Genesis 3:16** immediately after Adam and Eve ate of the forbidden fruit God, first, speaks to the woman:

To the woman He said: "I will greatly multiply your sorrow and your conception; In pain you shall bring forth children; Your desire *shall be* for your husband, And he shall rule over you."

This is the first time when a person was set above another person in what God is telling us - authority has now been manifested in the flesh and began to rule one over another. The thing is: God is saying this is a curse that has come upon us and not a blessing. God also mentions multiplying sorrow in child birth to teach us the value of His loving sovereignty is not something to be taken lightly.

This means that right from the beginning, the stage has been set to see which way is the best way:

Obedience to the Word of God which is manifested in humility to live in truth: the selfless ways of Christ.

Obedience to the Reprobate satan which is manifested in haughtiness to live in lies: the selfish ways of ego.

There is much confusion in the world today; and it is easy to see the reason why is because the 'selfish ways of ego' is continually striving to make the 'haughtiness to live in lies', which is personified as the noble search for truth in the name of science, is somehow acceptable.

While theories (of science) are pending verification, the prophecies (of scripture) are confirming the veracity of God's Word, and this goes a long way to prove things have not changed since the beginning; because it seems study after study has shown that societies that lack equality are proportionately ill and unhappy with the level of inequality that pervades that given society.

So we can keep our thoughts turned on what Christ did and said to discover the ineffable Hallowed Name of God.

Jesus tells us in Matthew 20:25-26 and John 15:15 (plus other areas in the Gospels) we are all to love one another equally and none are to raise their heads above another.

This sounds profoundly simple enough, and one would think it is easy to make this a reality. However, when we look at the back of a one dollar bill we see the 'image' of a hierarchy (power structure depicted as a pyramid) with the 'image' of an eye that seems to emanate rays of light.

This is the complete opposite of what Jesus describes - thus we can naturally conclude: hierarchy is the Image of the Beast and equality is the Image of God. When we look at things like this we can easily see how these compare when we observe the effect they have on people in any given society or situation:

In an environment where there are power structures people can plot and scheme to raise their head above others as they step on others to get on in life.

In an environment where there is equality and no one lusts for authority - love will flourish.

From this then we can see the Image of the Beast and the Image of God, and how they contrast. This also helps to understand why God said do not 'eat' of the forbidden fruit.

Scripture tells us in Ezekiel 3:1 – Moreover He said to me, "Son of man, eat what you find; eat this scroll, and go, speak to the house of Israel". Ezekiel was asked to digest the scroll which was filled with understanding and wisdom that establishes the Kingdom of God.

This means that the request by God, in the beginning to Adam and Eve to not partake of the forbidden fruit, is we must not digest the unholy knowledge that facilitates the building of the hierarchy (power structure). Thus we can see God wants us to take all necessary measures to not partake (eat to nourish the spirit) of this way of life to remain undefiled in His Hallowed Name.

God wants us to remain humble - no matter how tempting the life of power may appear to the eye.

Partaking (or eating) of the forbidden fruit, then, seems to mean accepting the hierarchy as good and pleasing that one can use to lust for and attain authority over others. In short, accepting the hierarchy is accepting the Mark of the Beast and if we do not accept the hierarchy we will receive the Mark of God.

There is talk of bringing in chips that the government want to insert under the skin, which people are saying is the Mark of the Beast - but we need to understand: this is the dragon trying to divert us from learning the Name of God.

Revelation doesn't only speak of wicked people receiving the Mark of the Beast on the forearm or forehead, but it also talks of virtuous people receiving the Image of God on the forearm or forehead too.

This means the marks people receive will not be placed on the forearm or forehead by man. It is something that will be divinely placed and these will only be visible to the avenging angels.

This then means we can turn our attention to how the Name of God is made visible.

Given the fact we are to advance in some way (through the Word sent by God) this means Christ was telling us He and the Father had the exact same Will, or to be more accurate He was telling us He had aligned His Will with the Father's Will as a perfect match. Jesus then goes on to say we are to emulate this same task by following His example because this will then fulfil God's plan to advance us in His image (as spoken of in the beginning).

This then means the divine plan is we are all to become One with the Father (through Christ) and given the Image of God is visible in each and every one of us who walks in the ways of God – the Glory of God can then fill the earth as prophesied.

This, then, is the visible Name of God because His Glory and His Name is One and the same thing – and Jesus was the first person to make this manifest on earth for all to 'see'.

To summarize what we have covered:

The Image of God = True Equality
True Equality = Glory of God (will soon cover the face of the earth)
Glory of God = His Eternal Ineffable (Observable) Name.

The Hallowed Name of God is an observable phenomenon and not something we can yet pronounce. This is what Yeshua HaMashiach (Jesus the Saviour) has revealed because the last commandment He gave was: 'Love one another as I also have loved you.'

He gave this commandment last - knowing only too well - it is the realization of this commandment that makes the Hallowed Name of God visible upon the face of the whole earth. This means we must look to one another to realize the visible presence of the Lord is His Glory that is manifested in the way we love each other.

Thus we are: **(In) the Name of God** – when we love one another as our beloved Christ also loved us.

For the time being we can use the Name YHWH (Yahweh) - knowing God has allowed it to be used because Jesus said ask the Father in my Name and you shall receive - and a time will come when Christ will utter the unpronounceable Name – and that is when we will see God with our very eyes.

Matthew 23:9 – Do not call anyone on earth your father; for One is your Father, He who is in heaven.

CAUSE AND EFFECT

OBSERVING THE TRUTH

Here is a picture of an Indian Chief ...or is it an Eskimo with a torch in the dark?

Hmmm...

If you look at the picture you can see both depending on how you allow your mind to concentrate on what you see with your eyes.

This is what scripture is like - it has the power to be seen two ways. One way leads to the truth - the other way leads to error - so a person reading scripture will either see what 'The Flesh' wants to see or what the 'Holy Spirit' wants see.

We only need to look at the church to see how scripture has been used to establish 'power structure' among the flock.

Christ told us in Matthew 20:26-28 not to do this.

What has happened with scripture through the centuries is: the people interpreting - translating or just reading it have failed to notice there is this dual aspect to understanding scripture and as such they ended up seeing only the one way.

...and this is the reason why (a) the church has apostatized and (b) scripture has survived through the centuries.

The first thing they (theologians) see is what they have assumed to be true and this is why things are as they are right now - with denomination after denomination trying to claim they are the true church of God.

How can any church claim to be in truth; if it cannot show how verses can be used to glorify God or glorify satan? Surely... the ability to discern the positive and the negative aspects in each verse is what distinguishes those who are in truth from those who are in error. This, then, is what qualifies a person to 'know' the truth when they can then show how such observation leads to the glorification of God.

The inability to see scriptural verses in this dual way is the stumbling block God said He would set in place before the haughty - and boy is it a powerful one too - I am in awe of this – but I do believe the time has come to reveal this to the world: because every minister – every individual –can secure the means by which they can see the path that is set before them.

With this knowledge, of how scripture is presented, you can develop the ability to see the path – which is about six inches wide with an abyss of demons clutching at your ankles as you make your way to paradise.

Take a look at the picture of the Indian / Eskimo (above) and notice how you can see both images at the same time - simultaneously.

Reading scripture, with the ability to see how the verses can be seen both ways (simultaneously) is - what I believe - to be the correct way to read scripture.

It takes practice to do this but when you fully develop the means to read in this way you will be working consciously with the Holy Spirit.

Otherwise, you are at the mercy of your own flesh (worldly understanding) to make any sense of the text you are reading and you run the risk of denying the Holy Spirit.

The following chapter will provide an example of how this can help make the correct conclusions to glorify God.

NOTES

_____

_____

_____

_____

_____

...OF LIGHTNESS OR DARKNESS

This book has outlined the means by which a person can ascertain how to glorify God or satan depending on the belief system that leads them to either break or keep the commandments as they walk in the faith they have.

It is clear any living human being on the planet has the opportunity to do either and the options are black and white. A person can either choose to:

1) Glorify God by loving their neighbour as themselves. This is best achieved by avoiding hierarchy or setting up any kind of hierarchy.

2) Glorify satan by worshiping anything that is not Yahweh. This is achieved by establishing or using an existing hierarchy.

This means, it doesn't matter if a person believes in science, leprechauns or false gods of the Pagan religions – including the false doctrines of the Christian denominations that profess to have the truth – each and every individual is responsible for the way they behave and their belief-system is what gives their behaviour impetus toward glorifying either God or satan.

Even if a person does not believe in satan they are still worshiping satan if they do not take care to reject the hierarchies that defile the Hallowed Name of God as and when appropriate.

There is one (classic) subject that highlights the way this can be seen, in its subversive manner, as we strive to learn how to discern the truth to walk the narrow path that leads to the Kingdom of God.

Let us consider the Trinity that has been used in Christianity for centuries to define the faith as we see it today in the modern churches.

Not many are aware that the Trinity is viewed in two ways. It can either be perceived as meaning Jesus the Christ is the Father in heaven who became flesh or it can be perceived as meaning Jesus the Christ is the Son sent by the Father who became the Word made flesh.

There is a reason why there are two ways to perceive this doctrine that has been polarized in this way, which will be covered later but for now it is important to clarify: on the one hand there is the belief Jesus is (literally) the Father (made flesh) and on the other hand there is the belief Jesus is the Word (made flesh).

Let us first of all consider the origin of the doctrine of the Trinity.

The concept of the Trinity has its origin in Babylon where the Pagans believed the Trinity was made of god the father, god the son and the mother of god who brought the god-son into the world.

This is the Pagan myth surrounding the birth of Mithra and it involves the son being born after the father who is also the son who impregnated the mother in what they believe was an immaculate conception of the virgin mother of god.

It seems totally unbelievable that people actually fell for this, but this is what they believed and this is where the concept of the Trinity originated. To cut a long story short, we need to leap forward to the time when this was used as a doctrine in the church we see today.

History records that Constantine saw a cross in the sky in a dazzling light and he instructed his troops to adopt the sign before they went into battle. This then is said to be the reason why Constantine became a Christian.

The truth is very different indeed. We have no way of knowing if Constantine actually had the vision he claimed to have had, but we do know that the cross is a Pagan symbol that goes back to the Babylonian era – and scripture (when accurately translated) records Christ was crucified on a pole or stake because the Romans were running so low on wood by the time Jesus was with us – they had little choice but to use a stake or pole. Some believe He was nailed to a tree but this is not recorded in scripture. This, then, means it is highly likely this 'pre-battle-vision' idea Constantine had was the excuse he needed to secure the Pagan symbol of the cross as a symbol of reverence for the Christian faith.

The cross was used before this time: but the fact remains it was introduced as a substitute for the pole or stake and it is highly likely it was deliberately introduced to obscure the two faiths of Paganism and Christianity into one that became known as Catholicism.

Matthew 10:38 – New King James Version (NKJV)

And whoever does not take his cross and follow me is not worthy of me.

The word 'cross' here is: G4716 – σταυρός – stauros – pronounced *stow-ros'*

From the base of G2476; a *stake* or *post* (as *set* upright), that is, (specifically) a *pole* (as an instrument of capital punishment); figuratively *exposure to death*, that is, *self denial*; by implication the *atonement* of Christ.

From this we can see the Christian faith has deliberately had key elements changed to falsify the doctrine that Christ taught to introduce Pagan symbols and doctrines. This can be seen by the way things transpired: Constantine passed a law that made Christianity the main religion of Rome but there are few who realised the New Emperor was a Pagan who had a political agenda behind the passing of this new law.

The truth is... Rome has remained Pagan as it sought to use Christianity as a front for their Pagan beliefs. The concept of the Trinity is one such doctrine that has been brought into the picture because it facilitates having a power structure.

So why has the word 'Trinity' been brought into the Christian churches?

Scripture never uses the word Trinity at all. All arguments that theologians use to try and verify the veracity of the Trinity are all inference and when they are faced with something that is inexplicable they resort to saying: "It's a mystery," or "If you do not believe in the Trinity, you will be damned."

God is not the author of confusion and **John 15:15** states: No longer do I call you servants, for a servant does not know what his master is doing; but I have called you friends, for all things that I heard from My Father I have made known to you.

This means there is no mystery that cannot be uncovered so it is not appropriate to state something is a mystery even if it is said to try and bring a discussion to an amicable close – inferring the intention to agree to disagree.

The answer is available; and this booklet will spell it out for the entire world to see:

When Rome split in two we saw the emergence of the Eastern Orthodox Church in Constantinople and the Holy Roman Catholic Church in Rome begin the debate over the concept of the Trinity and neither have come to a satisfactory conclusion.

The debate would lift verses from scripture that would show one way to be true and the opposition would show how the same words were not saying what the first said.

For example:

John 1:1 – New King James Version

In the beginning was the Word, and the Word was with God, and the Word was God.

The side that believe Jesus is the Father (made flesh) would say this clearly shows how John is saying Jesus is the Father (made flesh) because the verse states The Word (which is Jesus) was with God and the Word was God

Then the opposition, who believe Jesus is the Word (made flesh), would say the word God is the family surname; so it does not mean the Word is the Father and they would also add this particular verse mentions two personages so it cannot have any bearing on the Trinity argument.

This kind of thing went on and on for centuries and they still have not found a conclusive answer because people will usually choose on the balance of probabilities that are weighed up by the both sides or they would simply run with their gut instinct.

The thing is… where is the Holy Spirit during this debate?

Let us examine what happens when you place consider the belief in the two main viewpoints held over the Trinity and remaining focused on what glorifies God and which one glorifies satan in order to ascertain the truth.

The two options (for the foundation of the Christian faith) are:

1) Jesus is God the Son – who is the Father made flesh (Oneness Doctrine).
2) Jesus is the Son of God – who is the Word made flesh (God-Head Doctrine).

The obvious 'cause and effect' of the two types of beliefs can be outlined as follows because a Christian strives to be Christ-like:

Jesus Christ as God the Son – The Father Incarnate

If we are to be Christ-like, in the belief Jesus is the all powerful God the Son, we are buying into the idea that one person can be set above another. This is because we will be consciously striving to attain the power of God if we are to be Christ-like.

Jesus Christ as the Son of God – The Word Incarnate

If we are to be Christ-like, in the belief Jesus is the all humble Son of God, we are following all the commandments as laid down by God from the beginning. This is because we will be striving to attain the humility of Christ.

This then means we can look to the two beliefs and see which one glorifies God (allows people to be equal) and which one glorifies satan (allows people to set themselves one above another)

Given the 'fact' scripture can be interpreted to declare either belief to be correct we *must* look to these options in this fashion and accept the way they affect our behaviour because the only thing that is important is: the glorification of God.

Everything else is superfluous – because only the glorification of God matters.

John 16:7 – New King James Version (NKJV)

Nevertheless I tell you the truth. It is to your advantage that I go away; for if I do not go away, the Helper will not come to you; but if I depart, I will send Him to you.

This one single verse proves the three that make up the God-Head are one in purpose but they are separate in substance because Yeshua had to go to heaven before the Helper (Holy-Spirit) could come.

The most likely reason for this is because heaven must have at least two to bear witness at all times – as the law states there most be two to bear witness. Jesus clearly shows us how he must be with His Father (I must go away) so the Paraclete (Holy Spirit) may come to be with us.

The scripture is full of these ambiguous: this means that and that means this verses without giving clear indication which way is the correct way – because God specifically wanted to cause the haughty to stumble.

For example - Christ said: 'I and the Father are One'.

Oneness Doctrine believers will say this means Christ Himself is claiming He is the actual Father but it can also mean they are merely as one in purpose.

The Father, the Son and the Holy Ghost are (as) one in purpose – not substance. Yeshua – did live his life in complete obedience to God and showed us how God (the Father) would have lived if He had come in the flesh.

Here is the harsh truth:

The haughty lust for authority over others – so they will want to believe Christ is the all-powerful Father (made flesh) thus: that is what they will see in scripture.

The humble shun attaining authority over others – so they will want to believe Christ is the all-humble Word (made flesh) thus: that is what they will see in scripture.

One way glorifies God – the other glorifies satan.

You now know which is which so you have the means to know how to discern truth from lie and expose all the work of satan so you may become right with God.

Here is a list of doctrines I recommend you investigate:

Doctrine --- Area to Investigate

1) Christmas (Birth of Mithra) ----------------- Resurrection (Birth of Christ)
2) Easter --- Passover
3) Virgin Birth --------------------------------- Pure (clean) Birth (physical)
4) Trinity -- God-Head
5) Cross -- Pole or Stake
6) Born Again ------------------------------------ Spiritual Birth into Heaven

Then, there are other doctrines worth investigating such as the way grace has replaced the law (that is supposed to be written in the heart) or the way Yeshua HaMashiach should have no beard and short hair.

These are a small handful of doctrines that satan has used to obscure the truth and it is up to you to expose them for what they are.

NOTES

_____
_____
_____
_____
_____
_____
_____
_____
_____
_____
_____
_____
_____
_____
_____
_____
_____
_____
_____
_____

SO FAR... SO GOOD... SO WHAT NOW?

If you are wondering what to do now that you have read this booklet; Yeshua told us to continue going about or daily lives. This is (in part) because the power structures we see in our lives right now are with us whether we like it or not and the good Lord has found it to His advantage to make use of this as and when He has deemed necessary to do His will.

This book is not saying you should not try to better yourself – within a company but you should avoid hankering for power and if you are offered a position of greater responsibility which affords you more power. As long as you have not lusted for this position then you can accept it - because it may have been blessed by God.

On such occasions it would be wise to enter into prayer.

If you ever feel you are under spiritual attack – remember the words:

In the Name of Yeshua HaMashiach, I command all evil to depart from me.

James 2:8-10 – Revised Version (RV)

Howbeit if ye fulfil the royal law, according to the scripture, Thou shalt love thy neighbour as thyself, ye do well: but if ye have respect of persons, ye commit sin, being convicted by the law as transgressors. For whosoever shall keep the whole law, and yet stumble in one *point*, he is become guilty of all.

The reference here to 'respect of persons' means – if you partake of the hierarchy that glorifies satan in any way.

Thus, it is forbidden to take on the Image of the Beast.

Isaiah 62:2 – New King James Version (NKJV)

The Gentiles shall see your righteousness, and all kings your glory. You shall be called by a new name, which the mouth of the LORD will name.

NOTES

Philippians 2:5-11 – Good News Bible (GNB)

The attitude you should have is the one that Christ Jesus had: He always had the nature of God, but he did not think that by force he should try to remain equal with God. Instead of this, of his own free will he gave up all he had, and took the nature of a servant. He became like a human being and appeared in human likeness.

He was humble and walked the path of obedience all the way to death - his death on the *cross. For this reason God raised him to the highest place above and gave him the name that is greater than any other name.

And so, in honour of the name of Jesus all beings in heaven, on earth, and in the world below will fall on their knees, and all will openly proclaim that Jesus Christ is Lord, to the glory of God the Father.

* The word used for cross is 'stauros' which means - stake or pole (*not cross*).

NOTES

THE MESSAGE IN SCRIPTURE

Here is the message of the scripture for all to see. I have written them in first person - but the glory belongs to God for only the Father in heaven is good.

OLD TESTAMENT MESSAGE:

Behold, I am that I am have created you to be as I am in eternity but you have failed to respect the responsibility that comes with being as I am. It was for this reason I took the memory of you from you and made you to be as parents so you may come to respect the responsibility that comes with being as I am.

Whenever you feel joy or sadness as a result of your children being obedient or disobedient you share the same joy and sadness I feel when you are obedient or disobedient - even unto death. I am your father - call no one - but me - father that you may know how to respect the responsibility (keep the commandments) that comes with being as I am.

Then we shall walk together as equals in eternity - and to prove my sincerity - I shall send my son so you may come to remember who you are and know all I say is true.

NEW TESTAMENT MESSAGE:

Behold, I have sent my Son to teach you how to respect the responsibility that comes with being as I am. My Son has shown you how to walk with me as an equal and his words are clear for you to know:

1) If you do things 'to' others you are subject to the law.
2) If you do things 'for' others you are not subject to the law.

The flesh is not where you dwell and thus you are as I am when you love others as you love yourself. The blood of my Son gives you the opportunity to learn this truth and as you raise yourself to walk in my ways - you will become a living being born of spirit who Glorifies my Hallowed Name.

MESSAGE OF REVELATION:

A day will come when I am that I am shall walk among you as an equal because my Son has worked through the recent centuries to find overcomers to be as saints who have already come to know these things and lived their lives according to my ways.

The time is drawing near - and you are all my beloved children in whom I look forward to being with soon.

Peace be with you: always.

Selah